Kaija Saariaho

NoaNoa

for flute and electronics

Chester Music

NoaNoa was written for Camilla Hoitenga, who gave the first performance in Darmstadt on 23rd July 1992. She has recorded it on Ondine ODE 906–2. The work was realised in the Studios of IRCAM (musical assistant: Xavier Chabot).

Duration: c. 10 minutes

Software CD-ROM available on sale: Order No. OM 24564

INTRODUCTION

NoaNoa (Fragrant) was born in 1992 from ideas I had for flute while writing my ballet music *Maa*. I wanted to write down, exaggerate, even abuse certain flute mannerisms that had been haunting me for some years, and thus force myself to move into something new. Formally, I was experimenting with the idea of developing several elements simultaneously, first one after the other, then superimposed.

The title refers to a woodcut by Paul Gaugin called *NoaNoa*. It also refers to a travelling diary of the same name, written by Gaugin during his visit to Tahiti from 1891–93. The fragments of phrases selected for the voice part in the piece come from this book.

NoaNoa is also a team work. Many details in the flute part were worked out with Camilla Hoitenga. The electronic part was developed under the supervision of Jean-Baptiste Barrière, with Xavier Chabot as programmer.

K.S.

NoaNoa

l'arbre sen-tait la rose la rose très o-do-rant sen-tait rose rose sen-tait rose s t r t s t s t s t t t t t t
sen-tait la rose

mes-s yeux voi-lés par mon coeur-rr
sen-tait la rose la fleur-r
la...fleur

t t t t t t t très...odorant me-lange me-lange me-lange...d'odeur l'ar-bre sen-tait la rose fleur-r
tr tr tr

fleur fanée fleur fleur l f l f r
me-lange d'odeur par-fums par-fums de san-tal très...odorant s f tr f s z t f

l'arbre sentait
fleur...dorée Je...reviendrai
mes yeux yeux la fleur-r fleur fleur fleur fanée

t r t r t t t t t t t t t
je
fl sa tr t t t t t s t s t k s t k s t k s t k k tr ro je je t je t ta ka ta ka ro tr re fl sa ka tr s z t k z t k fl tr z t k ro fl tr
ka z t fl tr ro z t k fl tr z t k s t s
la...fleur
f r s t s s t s
la...fleur

Noa

Kaija Saariaho (1992)

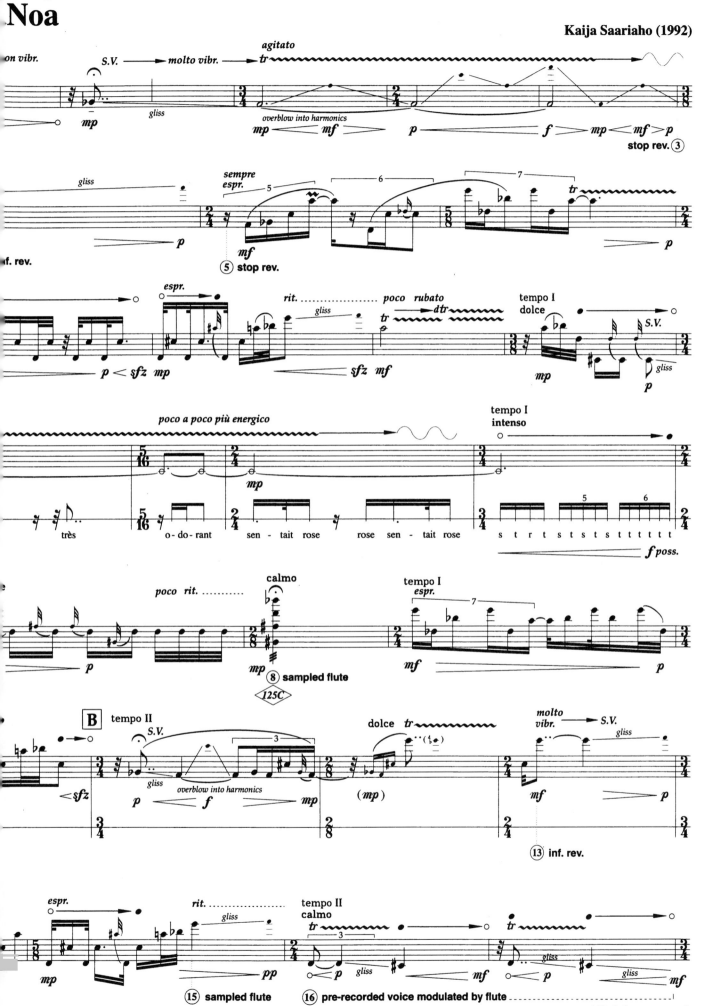

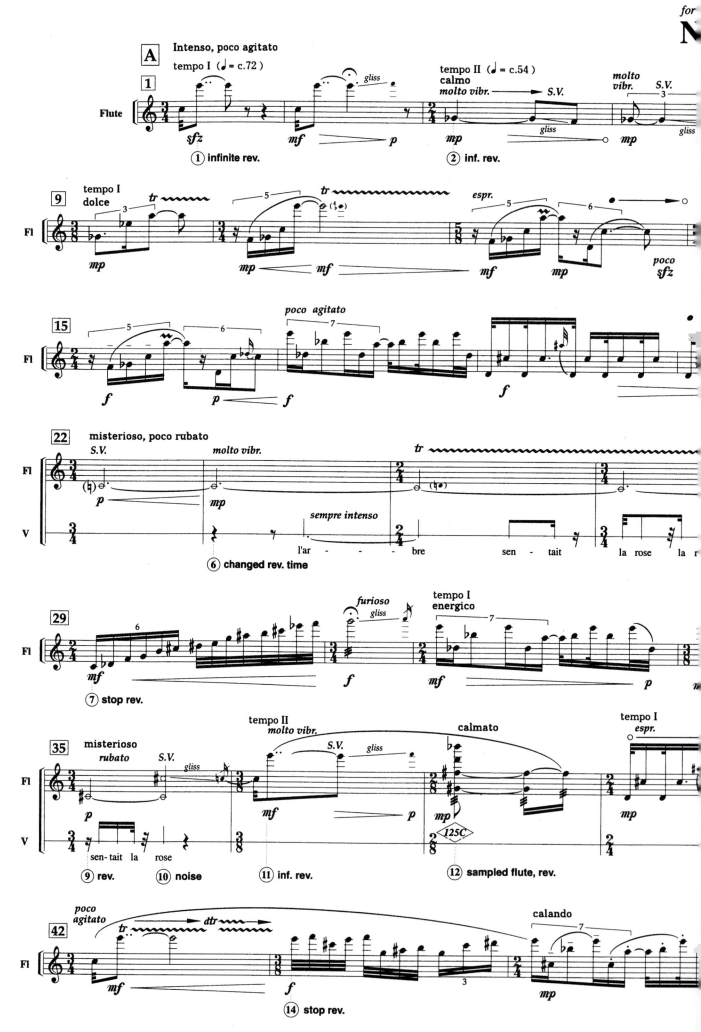

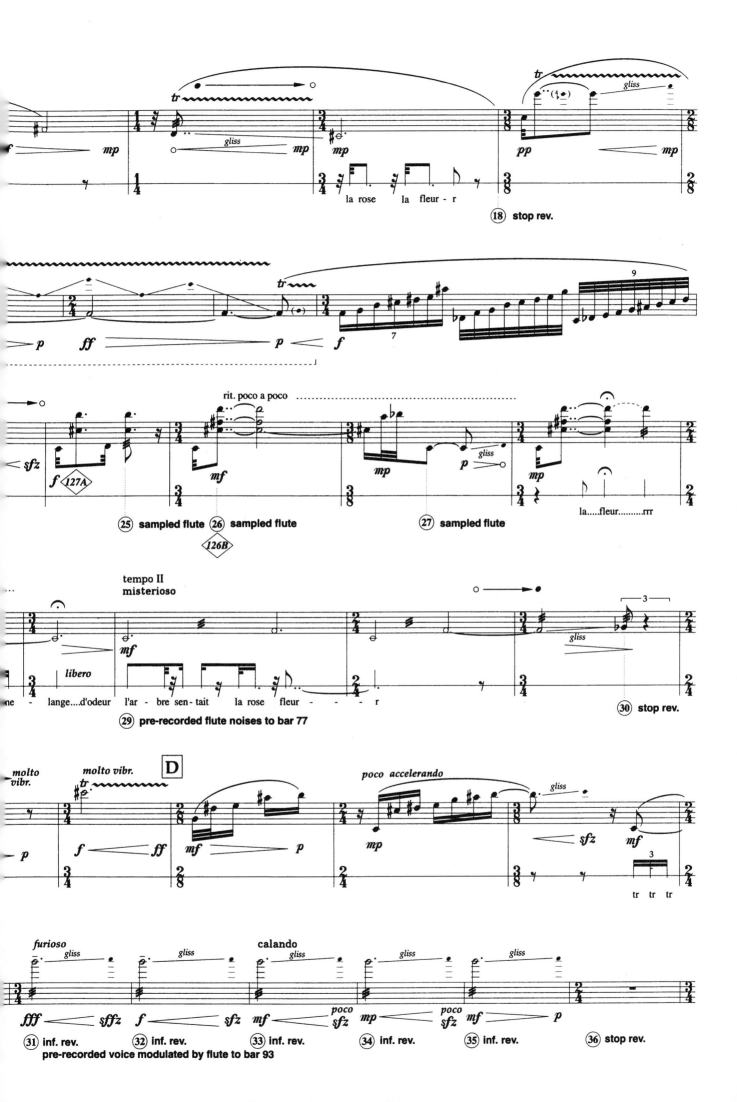

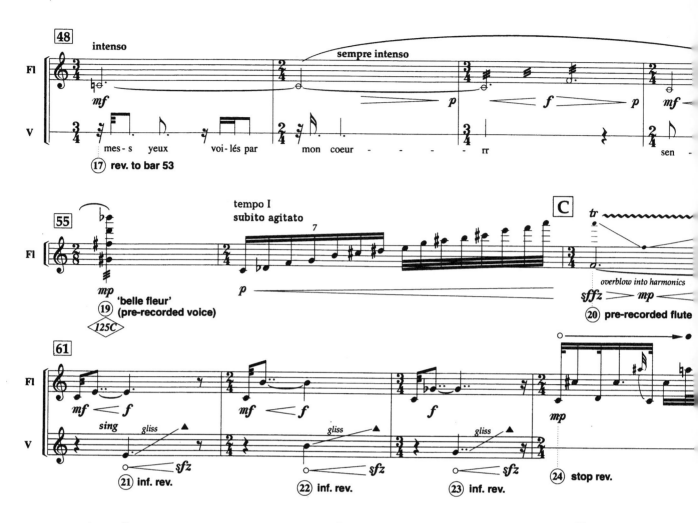

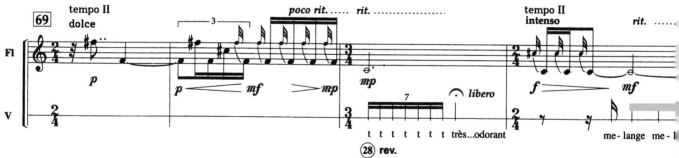

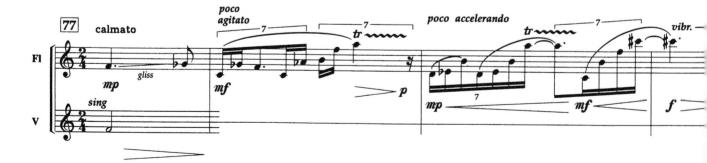

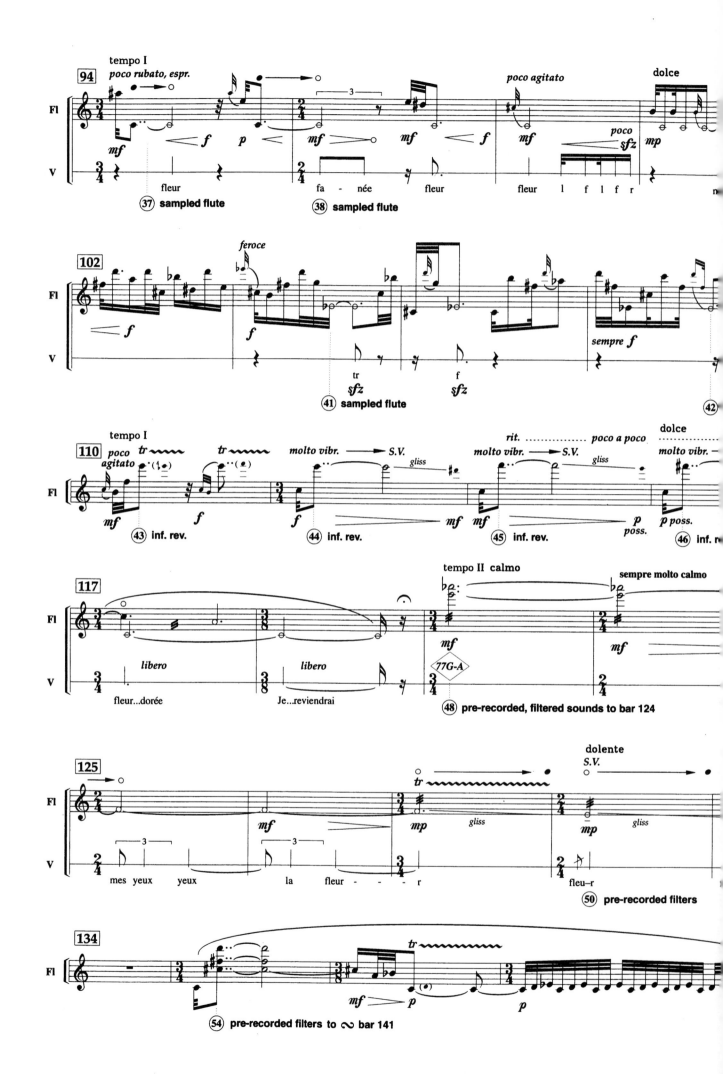

sffz — sa

sffz — tr

subito pp

t t t t t s t s t k s t k s t k s t k k — sffz

subito dolce

pp

subito feroce

dolce
tr

f — p

t je t — <sffz

ta ka ta ka ro tr — f poss.

re — sfz

) pre-recorded filters

(59) pre-recorded filters

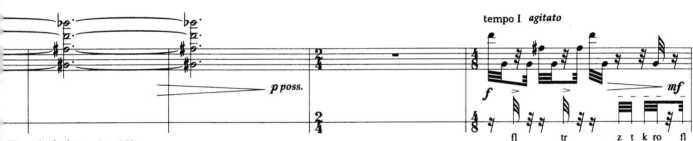

p poss.

tempo I agitato

f — mf

fl tr z t k ro fl

filters (voice) to ~ bar 159

p

tempo I

p — f

fl tr z t k s t s

rubato

dolcissimo

s s t s — la........fleur

ds

4

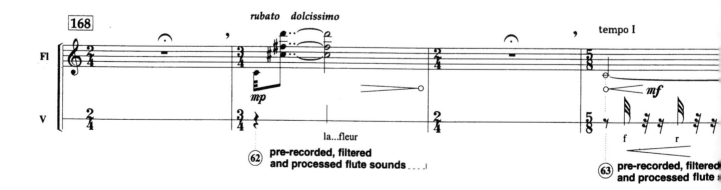

PERFORMANCE DATA

Equipment requirements – Macintosh version

–   Macintosh PowerPC with CD-ROM drive (compatible with system 7.1 or higher)

–   MIDI interface

–   1 Lexicon LXP-15 sound processor or Lexicon PCM80

–   1 general digital reverberation (a Yamaha SPX1000 or Lexicon PCM80
    or TC Electronics 5000 or equivalent)

–   1 sustain pedal (for triggering Max) connected to the Mac through any
    MIDI keyboard, or any device that converts voltage in MIDI

–   1– 2 microphones for the flute, mixer (2 sends), and PA with 2 high quality
    loudspeakers

All software (Max patches, as well as the samples) is installed on a CD-ROM, available from Chester Music.

The ideal sound for the amplification is a clear and rich "close" sound. The microphone should be placed rather close to the instrument. The amount of amplification naturally depends on the concert space, but the amplified sound should not cover the acoustic sound of the instrument. The general level can be set rather loud, but not painfully so.

The reverberation effect

The reverberation used in Lexicon LXP-15 consists of a program in which the reverb time is changed constantly by the amplitude of the input signal. The general idea here is: the quieter the sound, the longer the reverb. The amplified flute sound should blend well with the reverb sound, but nevertheless remain slightly in the foreground. The second reverb is used to soften the amplified flute sound, the Lexicon LXP-15 sound, and possibly the recorded audio material on direct-to-disk.

The performance situation

The instrumentalist triggers the changes in the LXP-15 effect and starts the pre-recorded audio material. The pedal changes are marked in the score with circled numbers ① – ㊻. A second person is needed to ensure a well-balanced mix between the different materials.

IMPORTANT NOTE: the technical information given above is correct as at September 1998, but performers should contact the publisher for updates.

NOTATION

Expression marks

$\longrightarrow$ change very gradually from one sound or way of playing (etc.) to another.

diminuendo al niente

crescendo dal niente

S.V.   senza vibrato

When vibrato markings are not specified, players can use their usual vibrato. "Molto vibrato" always means a rapid and narrow vibrato, unless otherwise specified. Tremolo should always be as dense as possible.

Micro-intervals

note raised a quarter tone (between ♮ and ♯).

note lowered a quarter tone (between ♮ and ♭).

d tr   double trill: trilling by quickly alternating the first and second finger of the right hand on the key that is normally trilled.

Unless otherwise marked, trills are always up a semitone, and glissandi are always semitone glissandi.

Articulations

breath tone: use the fingering needed to produce the marked pitch. Do not produce the normal tone, just blow air across the mouthpiece.

O   ●   breath tone: normal tone.

whisper the given phonemes into the instrument in the rhythm indicated, whilst simultaneously playing the pitches and other events as marked.

▲   as high as possible

Pronunciation

In general, pronunciation follows the rules of the French language, as follows:

d as in French <u>d</u>e	s as in French <u>s</u>oleil
f as in French <u>f</u>euilles	t as in French <u>t</u>oi
k as in French é<u>c</u>arté	zs as in French <u>j</u>aune
l as in French <u>l</u>e	etc.
r as in French mu<u>r</u>	

Always stress the phonemes, as though there were an accent on each of them.

Multiphonics

The numbers in diamond shaped boxes refer to P-Y Artaud's *Present Day Flutes* (Billaudot).